SoRting out

SELF-ESTEEM

DEDICATION

To my father Jack — a great mate.

SORting out SELF-ESTEEM

GRANT BRECHT

PRENTICE HALL

Sydney   New York   Toronto   Mexico   New Delhi
London   Tokyo   Singapore   Rio de Janeiro

Acquisitions Editor: Kaylie Smith
Production Editor: Elizabeth Thomas
Copy Editor: Loretta Barnard
Cover design: Eilish Bouchier
Ilustrations: David Egan

Typeset by DOCUPRO, Lane Cove, NSW

Printed in Australia by Australian Print Group,
  Maryborough, Victoria

1 2 3 4 5 00 99 98 97 96

ISBN 0 7248 1111 7

National Library of Australia
Cataloguing-in-Publication Data

Brecht, Grant Phillip
  Sorting out self-esteem

  Bibliography
  Includes index
  ISBN 0 7248 1111 7

  1. Self-esteem. 2. Self-actualization (Psychology).
  3. Motivation (Psychology). I. Title.
  (Series: Sorting out life series).

158.1

Prentice Hall of Australia Pty Ltd, *Sydney*
Prentice Hall, Inc., *Englewood Cliffs, New Jersey*
Prentice Hall Canada, Inc., *Toronto*
Prentice Hall Hispanoamericana, SA, *Mexico*
Prentice Hall of India Private Ltd, *New Delhi*
Prentice Hall International, Inc., *London*
Prentice Hall of Japan, Inc., *Tokyo*
Prentice Hall of Southeast Asia Pty Ltd, *Singapore*
Editora Prentice Hall do Brasil Ltda, *Rio de Janeiro*

PRENTICE HALL

A Division of Simon & Schuster

CONTENTS

PREFACE

Self-esteem, self-confidence and self-dignity are the foundations upon which the rest of our lives are built. Without healthy and solid levels of each we are very vulnerable to the disorders of everyday living which can severely interfere with our quality of life. Guilt, anxiety and fear are very ready to accept the person with low self-esteem as fair game.

Some people appear to have been born with a great self-image and plenty of confidence in their own ability. They capitalise on the good times in their life and deal with adversity with a level of challenge and energy that is awe inspiring. Of course they were not born that way! They developed certain attitudes, beliefs, thinking styles and behaviours which they formulated into a very positive habit; a habit of looking at what they can do in life and of what they have done and then building on this. A habit of accepting their fallibilities, and mistakes in life, and formulating action plans to do better next time.

A solid foundation of high self-esteem enables us to build a solid lifestyle — relationships, career, parenthood, sporting achievements and any other aspects of living that we value.

Without a high level of self-esteem, all these other aspects of our life are on a shaky foundation and can too easily fall down around us. A healthy self-esteem leads to quick and effective decision-making, and ability to deal with all sorts of change in life and to stick up for our own rights and what we believe in.

This book in the *Sorting Out* series will show you how to recognise high or low self-esteem by yourself, how to develop healthy levels of self-esteem, and how to recognise when you are successful in that endeavour. It will also assist you if you are living with someone with low self-esteem. Enjoy boosting your self-esteem, and developing an attitude that says 'I am important'.

Grant Brecht

ACKNOWLEDGMENTS

My sincere gratitude to all who have been encouraging and of assistance in the endeavour to produce this series of books. My appreciation to the many psychologists from whom I have drawn both knowledge and inspiration. Thank you to Kaylie Smith from Prentice Hall for your guidance and enthusiasm for the overall project. Special thanks to Dr John Lang for his assistance in my final realisation that with a desire, focus and "stick-ability", anything in life is truly possible.

Thanks to Lyn and Oliver for ongoing support and tolerance of my efforts to accomplish a goal. Will I ever forget the words of one gorgeous five year old boy 'You're not working on those books again are you Daddy?'

ABOUT THE AUTHOR

Grant Brecht is a Clinical Psychologist who works and lives in Sydney, Australia. He is a sought-after presenter and speaker who is well known for his radio and television appearances, assisting people to sort out their lives.

Grant is the Director of CORPsych—a psychological consultancy providing counselling and training services to companies and individuals across Australia and New Zealand. Grant has a unique ability to impart information and assist people to learn psychological self-help techniques in a very practical and enjoyable manner.

Look for other books by Grant Brecht in the *Sorting Out* series.

ABOUT THE SERIES

A wise person once remarked that 'Life is not about having no problems, but rather about being able to resolve them quickly when they occur'.

The *Sorting Out* series of books has been written to assist each of us to do just that—to sort out those everyday life challenges that confront everyone of us. Whether it be ongoing and unnecessary worry and anxiety, an inability to plan and set goals in life, low self-esteem and a poor self-image or too many perceived demands with too few coping strategies, the books in this series will be of immense practical value and benefit.

Our modern lifestyles are demanding and the rapid rate of social and technological change is placing unprecedented pressures on all of us. Quality of life is determined by how well we predict and rise to the challenges which are placed before us on our journey through life. Our ability to communicate effectively is paramount. Effective communication is about remaining flexible, adaptable, rational, positive and solution-orientated no matter what is happening in our lives.

This very practical and relevant series of books will assist everyone in developing awareness of the issues and topics covered: how we know if it is a problem for us, including the signs and symptoms, and what we can do about it; how we know when we are successful and where to seek further assistance if we need to; and how to live with someone with that particular concern or problem.

The techniques and self-help procedures in the series are drawn from the latest research into the most effective approaches for dealing with the problems and hassles of everyday living.

CHAPTER 1

Self-esteem — what is it?

I looked in the mirror and liked what I saw
I looked once again and liked it even more.

Brecht 1995

How many of us look in the mirror and actually like what we see? I guess it is probably the ultimate test of self-esteem and our own self-image. Don't make the mistake of supposing that this means we have an over-inflated ego, or that we get carried away by a sense of self-importance.

If we give ourselves a pat on the back or look in that mirror and say 'Hey, I like you', we tend to feel we are getting carried away. However, this could not be further from the reality of what a healthy self-esteem and self-image is really all about. Still, it is the way many of us tend to think. So what do we do? We tend to look in the mirror and say 'Oh no, not you again — a bit drab, boring and uninteresting'. Then we shrink away from the mirror, feeling dull, boring and uninteresting. Some of us, of course, run away from the mirror screaming in agony at what we have just been exposed to — ourselves.

It's sad, but true. How many of us have actually sat down recently and written out a list of our good points — those things that we do well, that we are good at, the nice aspects of our personality, the last nice thing we did for someone else?

Why do we need a very healthy level of self-esteem? Why is it so important for us?

HINT NO.1 SELF-ESTEEM IS THE FOUNDATION THAT WE BUILD THE REST OF US ON

Yes, it's crucial alright, and yet we pay so little attention to it so much of the time. If our self-esteem is brittle, lacking or in general poor shape, everything else about us is likely to follow suit and be in the same state of disrepair. How can we be assertive about our rights in life, make decisions that suit us, and run successful relationships with other people if we are unsure and self-doubting? Of course, the answer is that we can't!

HINT NO. 2 SELF-ESTEEM IS ALL ABOUT LIKING OURSELVES, WARTS AND ALL

We have to learn to accept our fallibilities, and be able to get on with life, giving it our best shot. Easier said than done? So is playing tennis until you start to practise it on a regular basis. Maybe having a very healthy level of self-esteem is no different — we just need to practise doing the things that enhance our self-esteem on a regular basis. It works for almost everything else in life, so why not self-esteem?

Perhaps a lot of it is about focusing. If we choose to focus on what we can't do in life and what we don't have, of course we will demotivate ourselves, our self-esteem and self-confidence will take a real dive. However, if we choose to focus instead on what we can do, and what we have done in life and build on that, our self-esteem is likely to take a positive surge forward or at a least maintain a healthy level.

HINT NO. 3 YOU CAN LEARN TO ENHANCE YOUR SELF-ESTEEM

Self-esteem is something we develop as we travel the journey of life. Some of us will develop high self-esteem, feel content and at ease with who, and what we are. Others of us will have very brittle self-esteem and we can remain anxious and ill at ease because of this. If you are experiencing the second situation described, *don't panic*. Reading this book will help you to overcome your low self-esteem and to feel good about yourself and who you are. If you feel your self-esteem is already at a healthy level, then the book will be useful to use as a check to make sure all is okay and to ensure your self-esteem remains high as you travel through life.

HINT NO. 4 YOU CAN MAINTAIN HIGH SELF-ESTEEM FOR LIFE

This really is the good news. Once you understand what self-esteem is, and how to attain it, there is no reason that you need ever go back to a situation where your self-esteem is brittle for any substantial period of time. Maintaining a healthy level of self-esteem is like maintaining anything else in life. We need to *practise* regularly those things that keep our level of esteem high. This is no different to wanting to be good at a particular sport, a subject at university or a career. The more we practise, the more effective we become and the more payoffs we get from what we are doing.

HINT NO. 5 A HEALTHY LEVEL OF SELF-ESTEEM IS ONE OF THE GREATEST GIFTS WE CAN GIVE OUR CHILDREN, OR MODEL FOR OTHER PEOPLE

A well-known American psychologist, Dr Martin Seligman, author of *Learned Helplessness* and *Know What You Can Change, Know What You Can't*, has done a lot of research into depression and depressive disorders. He found a direct link between parents who were pessimistic, cynical and negative, and children who grew into young adulthood with major depressive disorders. So, if we expose our children to a good healthy dose of high self-esteem from ourselves, it appears they benefit from it in many ways, not the least of which is that you are teaching and showing them how to develop those behaviours and attitudes in life which lead to good levels of self-esteem in themselves.

WHAT IS SELF-ESTEEM?

I have been talking about why we need self-esteem and how it is good for us and have not yet provided a definition of what self-esteem actually is. Now there's a good test of self-esteem, to be able to accept that you have done something backwards!

Self-esteem is the acceptance of ourselves, by ourselves, for who and what we are at any time in our life. It is associated with the belief that we are worthwhile, capable and useful no matter what has happened in our life, what is happening, or what may happen.

Self-esteem is identified by the way we act and behave, by the attitudes and beliefs we hold about ourselves and the way we feel about ourselves and the emotions we experience. It is about developing and keeping a very positive self-image.

When we have a healthy and high level of self-esteem, we hold ourselves in high regard, we like and accept who we are, we forgive ourselves easily, we focus on our strengths and we can effectively distinguish ourselves from our behaviour or what we do. Then, if we make a mistake or mess something up, we still acknowledge that we are okay, that it was that particular thing we did that was no good or did not work. It's when we find ourselves saying things like 'I'm hopeless and useless because I made a mistake', that we are probably exhibiting symptoms of low self-esteem. Life can then become a self-fulfilling prophecy, where our lifestyle is one in which we think and act in a hopeless and helpless manner.

Self-esteem is the ability to look at what we can do, and what we have done, and build on this during our lives, rather than looking at what we haven't done and what we can't do, and filling ourselves up with blame and self-doubt. Self-esteem is also about setting our own goals and directions in life and not having to act in a particular way or do things too often just to get approval from others. It is about being able to say 'I don't care what the Joneses have, I will do my best to get what I want in life'. It is the ability to accept that other people will be able to do things better than we can, will have more money, may have more friends and may have more opportunities than we do. The ability to come second, third, fourth, or not even get a place, with dignity and acceptance is a sure sign of high self-esteem, as is the ability to accept coming first with confidence and dignity.

Put in a nutshell, self-esteem is the ability to accept what we drew in the lottery of life, the ability to persevere at those things we have a chance of influencing and to accept those things we have no control over. As the book progresses, you will develop a very good understanding of what self-esteem is all about.

SUMMARY

◆ Liking yourself is the foundation for a high quality of life.

◆ Hints on why we need a healthy level of self-esteem:
   1. Self-esteem is the foundation that we build the rest of us on.
   2. Self-esteem is all about liking ourselves, warts and all.
   3. You can learn to enhance your self-esteem.
   4. You can maintain high self-esteem for life.
   5. A healthy level of self-esteem is one of the greatest gifts we can give our children, or model for other people.

DEFINITION OF HIGH SELF-ESTEEM:

◆ The acceptance of ourselves by ourselves for who, or what we are, at any time in our lives.

◆ We need to consider what we have done and what we can do, not just what we haven't done and what we can't do.

CHAPTER 2

How do I know if I have it?

Knowing what self-esteem is provides a great foundation for the next step, which is knowing whether you have a good healthy chunk of it! Some of us worry that too much self-esteem could be a very bad thing to have. We may think that we will become, or appear to be, conceited and that others will find us rather difficult to be around due to the fact we will be continuously 'big noting' ourselves. In other words, we associate high levels of self-esteem with being a big deal. Not so! People with high self-esteem will talk and act in a confident manner and will certainly put their point of view forward if they feel it is required or necessary. You do not have to be 'away with the fairies', you can go about your everyday business in a relaxed and quiet manner without drawing any attention to yourself if that is the way you would like it. You can be quietly confident if you wish.

People who have problems with other people who have high levels of self-esteem are generally those who have low self-esteem and are looking for excuses as to why they are not that confident themselves! Another interesting characteristic of people with a good self-concept is that they can deal with failure, and admit when they are wrong. Both of these things can be very difficult for many of us to deal with. When things don't go as we like or we make a mistake, it is a common practice for us to start 'beating ourselves up' emotionally and attitudinally.

We can tell ourselves that we are hopeless and useless and

really quite stupid. The reality, of course, is that *you* are not stupid or hopeless; *your behaviour* and actions may have been at that time, but it certainly does not make you stupid or hopeless. People with high self-esteem make the distinction between the two because they realise that if you tell yourself you are stupid too often, you begin to act more and more that way, which is really very unfortunate. These people say 'What *I did* at that time was pretty silly' — they do not say that *they* are silly. Keep in mind that there are a million ways to lower our self-esteem if we are not ever vigilant and alert.

Self-esteem for human beings is like the foundations for a house. It is the important structure that everything else is built on. If a house has faulty foundations, whatever is built on top of them will be less than secure. The house will remain vulnerable, and even a very mild earth tremor could have quite disastrous effects. It is the same with ourselves. If we have a rather shaky self-esteem and self-concept, then anything we do to develop ourselves in life will be built on very brittle foundations. So when we fail at something, or something does not go as we had hoped it might, we tell ourselves how hopeless and useless we are and our self-esteem takes a real battering. So, too, can our overall quality of life because we don't feel good about ourselves.

Let's review what your self-esteem *foundations* are like, and in particular, whether they are adequate enough to stand the knocks that other people and life in general can deliver at times.

A SELF-ESTEEM QUIZ

Please rate the following questions	
Not at all like me	0
A little like me	1
Quite a bit like me	2
Very much like me	3
Exactly like me	4

1. I know I am a worthwhile person. _____
2. I regularly give myself a 'pat on the back'. _____
3. The goals I set in life are very much my own. _____
4. I know I will achieve my goals in life. _____
5. I criticise my actions, not myself. _____
6. Trying new things in life is very stimulating for me. _____
7. I allow myself to make mistakes in life. _____
8. I enjoy and seek out the company of very positive people. _____
9. I tend to stick up for my rights and needs in life. _____
10. I have many successes I remember in my past. _____

Interpreting your profile:

0–10 This book is timely reading for you. You are certainly not doing yourself any favours at the moment. The old 'kick butt' mentality to try to motivate ourselves is a fallacy. You need to start catching yourself being good and give yourself more pats on the back. Start by considering what you can do, and build on that. Never mind what you can't do. Slowly learn to do it by telling yourself positive things about your achievements, no matter how small. More advice and assistance for you later in the book.

11–20 I know what it's like! The twilight zone — neither here nor there. If your score is up near the 20 end, you are on your way, but not quite there. There's room to increase your own self-concept to ensure you weather the tough times well.

21–30 Well done. Your foundations are pretty solid, and you have an attitude that says 'I am important to look after and that's what I am going to do'. It will be helpful for you to have a look at your answers again to see if there were any areas that you need to be watchful about. Some of these areas could in fact start to erode your self-esteem if you allowed them to.

31–40 Excellent. This indicates a very healthy level of self-esteem. This area of your life is a real strength for you so make sure you keep it that way! It is a very important area of consideration in your life and you are doing well. It's great to see people orientated to giving life their best shot, so keep it up.

If your score was lower than you liked, don't panic, that's probably why you are reading this book. The following chapters will show you how to build and maintain a far healthier level of self-esteem and self-confidence. Often it is not as hard as we may imagine. Like anything else in life the key is generally *to practise*. Then to practise, practise and practise some more. It's no different from learning to type well or play tennis well.

BOUNCING BACK

One way to consider your self-esteem is to see how well you bounce back from disappointment, failure or any form of set-back in your life. Following these sorts of events occurring in life, do you tend to:

◆ withdraw;

◆ blame others;

◆ develop a 'poor me' attitude;

◆ get quite depressed;

◆ consume too much alcohol;

◆ eat too much; or

◆ give up?

Or are you the type who certainly gets a little emotional, and then:

◆ analyses what went wrong and tries to fix it;

◆ says 'I'm okay, my actions were wrong in that instance';

◆ plans a step-by-step recovery;

◆ keeps a good balance in your life, no matter what the circumstances?

SUMMARY

◆ Having high self-esteem is not the same as being a 'big deal'.

◆ High self-esteem enables you to interact with others in a confident manner.

◆ Self-esteem is the foundation for all future self-development.

◆ What conclusions do you draw from your self-esteem quiz profile?

◆ Following disappointment, failure or set-backs, do you become negative and demotivated, or do you accept, refocus and look for a solution?

CHAPTER 3

Where do you get it from?

Wouldn't it be great if you could actually order self-esteem through the mail and have it arrive the next day! Or perhaps take a self-esteem pill! It certainly would be convenient. But, of course, it's not that simple or easy to acquire healthy levels of self-esteem. If you had the right parents, you would be off to a good start.

I will explain the role that our parents had in the development of our self-esteem, because it is important to know where self-esteem comes from, so that you can start to control, keep controlling well or control a bit better those areas that are within your control. It is also important to understand those contributors to self-esteem that are not within our control so that we can understand them, accept them and get on with the task of developing a high level of self-esteem.

When we are unsure of how to go about improving our levels of self-esteem, if we are not happy with it, or when we feel we have low self-esteem because of others, we can very easily fall into a Victim Trap. This is most unfortunate because a vicious cycle may be set up.

We will learn all about the Victim Trap in the next few chapters. Now it's time to consider where our present level of self-esteem came from.

PARENTS

Parents are a great source of high or low self-esteem in children. With the best of intentions, many very caring and loving parents go about ripping the self-esteem from their children, never really understanding what they are doing. Although these days there are some very good parenting courses and workshops available, few parents avail themselves of the opportunity. We tend not to see such courses as important, compared, say, with vacuuming the house, working on the extension or spending a few more hours at work.

I firmly believe, having practised for many years as a psychologist, that the greatest gift a parent can give their children is to enhance their self-esteem, self-dignity and self-confidence levels.

SORTING OUT SELF-ESTEEM

Parents can enhance self-esteem in many ways, by:

◆ noticing when the child is being good;

◆ criticising behaviour, not the child;

◆ allowing the child to make mistakes;

◆ rewarding effort, not just outcome;

◆ plenty of hugs, cuddles and saying 'I love you';

◆ showing an interest in what the child is doing;

◆ encouraging mixing with other children;

◆ providing variety in his or her lifestyle;

◆ letting the child win quite often.

Parents can contribute to lowering self-esteem by:

◆ saying things like 'I hate you . . . you always do the wrong thing . . . you're an awful child';

◆ continually catching the child being bad;

◆ rescuing the child from all situations they do not like;

◆ the parents themselves being negative, cynical and pessimistic;

◆ criticising the child rather than the behaviour;

◆ not giving enough praise for effort, only for 'top marks';

◆ always having to be right, and having the last say;

◆ bullying the child;

◆ restricting the child's life experiences;

◆ setting the child up as a scapegoat;

◆ trying to motivate the child by comparing them with their siblings.

These lists are obviously not exhaustive, however they do allow you to consider your own family circumstances and how it may have contributed to your present level of esteem. This is not an opportunity to *blame* or heap a *guilt* trip on your parents. This is an unfortunate and quite naive response. Many people grew up in families where self-esteem was not high on the agenda.

Many have gone on to develop very healthy levels of it and have a very high quality of life. This is one of those areas that is really quite uncontrollable, so we need to 'cop it sweet' as they say. We have to understand that while it may have contributed to our low self-esteem, we do not have to remain like that. We need to understand and then move on to be how we would like to be.

CASE STUDY

Jean, a 21 year old Arts student, found it difficult to talk up and join in her tutorial discussions. She felt that what she had to say was not as important or interesting as the information from her fellow students. Jean was also worried that the other students would think she was silly and naive. Jean's tutor recommended a counsellor to help Jean overcome her anxieties.

It transpired that Jean had grown up in a family with an older sister who was a very high achiever. Jean was an average student. To try and motivate Jean, her parents constantly pointed out how well her sister was doing and that Jean could not possibly do as well. They were trying to shame her into working harder. Instead, Jean grew up believing she was second rate — not as good as her sister or other people.

Later chapters in the book will explain what you can do to develop or enhance your self-esteem levels if they are down and you feel your family circumstances may have contributed to this.

PEERS AND FRIENDS

The people who you mix with can have a very real effect on how much self-esteem you end up with at any time in your life. If you are in primary school and other kids tease you about your new glasses, your self-esteem may be brittle for a while until the glasses are no longer a novelty. The effect that such behaviour has on you will determine how long the effects last. Getting braces or having pimples as a young teenager may also see your friends 'turn' on you for a while. The effect this will have on you depends on your level of self-esteem. If you have to dress a certain way and act a certain way to stay in the 'gang' this may also actually erode self-esteem.

Self-esteem can be enhanced greatly by a group of friends who accept you just for being you. If your peer group looks up to you for what you have achieved, or sees you as an expert at something, this will also help to boost your self-esteem level. If you are recognised and acknowledged by others as being good at something, this can do wonders for your self-esteem.

ACHIEVEMENTS

If you have developed a pattern of achieving in life, in a number of major areas, you are likely to believe that you can do things, that you are okay, and you feel really good about yourself. As the old saying goes 'nothing succeeds like success'.

The ability to set realistic and achievable goals in life and to pat ourselves on the back for every step we make towards them is also a great self-esteem booster. Common areas for achievement include: work, study, sports, community and voluntary activities, relationships, wealth, leisure and recreational pursuits.

YOURSELF

Without a doubt, the most important source of self-esteem is yourself. You can lower or bolster your own self-esteem whenever you feel like it. People who have healthy levels of self-esteem:

- look at what they can do and what they have done;
- give themselves regular pats on the back;
- criticise their behaviour, not themselves ('that was a silly thing to do', rather than 'I'm a silly person for doing it');
- ask for pats on the back from others;
- stick up for themselves.

People who are their own worst enemy:

- look at what they can't do and what they haven't done;
- criticise themselves rather than their behaviour or actions;
- are cynical, negative and pessimistic;
- set unrealistic goals that are almost impossible to achieve;
- think because they feel silly they are silly and run on feelings or emotions;
- think that having high self-esteem means you think you are a big deal.

WHERE DOES IT COME FROM? — A CHECKLIST

Spend a few minutes thinking about the following areas of your life and note down what positives and negatives you feel were, or are, there in relation to helping or hampering your self-esteem.

PARENTS: THINGS THEY DID OR STILL DO

Positives	Negatives
_____	_____
_____	_____
_____	_____
_____	_____

SORTING OUT SELF-ESTEEM

PEERS/FRIENDS

Positives	Negatives

WORK

Positives	Negatives

SPORTS/LEISURE/RECREATION: WHAT HAVE YOU ACHIEVED?

Positives	Negatives

YOURSELF: HERE'S THE BIG ONE! HOW DO YOU CONTRIBUTE TO YOUR OWN SELF-ESTEEM?

Positives	Negatives

OTHER: ANYTHING ELSE THAT YOU FEEL AFFECTS YOUR LEVEL OF SELF-ESTEEM

Positives	Negatives
_____	_____
_____	_____
_____	_____
_____	_____

So these are some of the major areas where your present level of self-esteem comes from. As you can see, some are extrinsic or external to ourselves, and others are intrinsic or from within us. Both are important. We need to be our own best friend and talk positively and encouragingly to ourselves while doing things and placing ourselves in situations that are rewarding and which provide us with good experiences.

SUMMARY

◆ No quick fix to give you high self-esteem.

◆ Beware the Victim Trap and low self-esteem cycle.

◆ Where does it come from?
  parents;
  peers;
  achievements;
  ourselves.

◆ External and internal sources of self-esteem are important.

CHAPTER 4

What gets in the way of it?

Barriers, barriers and more barriers! We saw some of the barriers to developing high self-esteem in the previous chapter. There seem to be many barriers in our lives, but we should not lose sight of the fact that there are also a huge number of opportunities. But if we are not alert and careful, there are quite a few things that can get in the way of you developing plenty of that important commodity — self-esteem.

We will be looking at a number of the barriers to self-esteem, but there is one in particular that is extremely important to be aware of, so that you can do something about it if it is a real block to boosting your self-esteem. That barrier is the Victim Trap. This was mentioned in the previous chapter, and it's a very nasty trap. Not only does it have a very detrimental effect on you personally, but it can affect many other people around you as well. So please pay particular attention to the section in this chapter which describes what the Victim Trap is all about. Self-esteem can be had and lost. Because we have a very high level at one time in our life does not mean we have it for life. We need to keep monitoring ourselves and track how we are going with this important quality of life issue.

Let's look at what can get in the way of us feeling great about ourselves, happy to be who we are. The first one is obvious.

NEVER HAD IT

Having read the first three chapters, you should now have a fairly good idea as to whether you ever had or still do have reasonable levels of self-esteem. From the previous chapter, you should have gained a clearer idea of why you have it or don't have it! So if you were brought up in a family where you were fairly continuously put down, then you will probably not have developed good self-esteem and that of course is a barrier for you now. You need to learn how to get self-esteem, and *you will* get it if you want to. Remember that you're important to look after.

Once you have low self-esteem, you can actually begin to live out a life script which says 'I'm hopeless', 'I can't do anything worthwhile'. It's as if we have written a negative script for our life play in much the same way as a playwright would write a script for any other play. Once the script is written, and practised ('I'm a hopeless, useless human being, everybody is better than I am') we then go about acting it out in real life. We don't stand up for ourselves, we do things to please others not ourselves, we don't take risks, we find it difficult to make decisions and generally reach about 10 per cent of our possible potential.

This is sad, because it does not need to happen. Yet if we allow our past, and things that happened back there to be a barrier to our present and our future, it will happen. Later chapters will show you how to break down these barriers if they exist within you.

HAD IT AND LOST IT

Self-esteem, self-confidence and our sense of self-dignity can drop right away from us. We end up frightened to have a go at other things. This of course happens when we react negatively to a failure or a mistake in our lives and react as if that were a catastrophe — 'It's terrible, what a mess, I can't stand it, I shouldn't have . . .'.

The drop in confidence we experience, coupled with the anxiety and fear of making the same or another mistake, can become a barrier to us getting on with achieving other things and raising our self-esteem back up. The old 'what if?' syndrome kicks in here and we talk ourselves into a real mess, and at the end of it all, tell ourselves how hopeless we are. People actually become terrified of the symptoms of failure, such as depressed feelings and the sense of 'what's life all about?', and so avoid situations where this could occur. Once again, the end result is continuing low self-esteem.

THE VICTIM TRAP

This is a *very common* self-imposed trap that many people fall into.

The beauty of it, of course, is that because it is self-imposed we can do something about it if we desire. Once people have been in the Victim Trap for a while, they develop a definite *victim mentality* which is full of all sorts of irrational and distorted thinking patterns and beliefs. The most obvious sign of people who have the Victim Trap as a barrier to high self-esteem is the continual tendency to *project blame out* onto other people or other things. This is their excuse as to why they cannot and do not feel good about themselves.

CASE STUDY

Thomas, a 31 year old sales executive, missed out on the sales manager's position for which he had applied. He immediately put this down to the fact that he did not get involved in the politics in the company and so was not one of the 'boys'. Thomas began to feel quite despondent, lost motivation and his work performance suffered. For the next three months he failed to reach his monthly sales target. His manager eventually called him in to discuss the decline in his performance. Thomas did not discuss how he was feeling or why he had lost his enthusiasm. Inwardly he still blamed the company for not realising his value. He did not speak to anyone about why he did not get the job. A fortnight later Thomas resigned, without having another job to go to. He was unemployed for five months.

The reason Thomas did not get the job was because another applicant had a five-year successful history of managing a large sales team. Thomas was being considered for a senior sales executive role until the decline in his performance.

A symptom of the Victim Trap is that the person has, or develops, what psychologists call an *external locus of control*. In ordinary English, this means projecting blame out onto others as the reason why things are not going well in their lives. This leads to negative and irrational thinking.

NEGATIVE AND IRRATIONAL THINKING

'It's their fault I don't feel good about myself, they made me feel depressed.' Rather than do something constructive about the situation, so that we can feel good about the fact that we have tried to solve it, we just pour forth with negative and upsetting self-talk and irrational thinking.

LACK OF PLEASANT EVENTS

Because we are so negative we always look for what is wrong with the things we are involved in. We lose our enjoyment because we are so critical and cynical, and only see the dark side. This can then lead to a sense of hopelessness.

SENSE OF HOPELESSNESS

This is a belief that things are out of our control and must be left up to fate, so nothing good is likely to happen to us. Once we start believing this sort of thing we stop involving ourselves and stop participating in things, and once again the ability to get positive feedback about ourselves and what we are doing is diminished. The picture is pretty clear. We are starting to set up a fairly vicious little circle of failure and low self-esteem.

DEPRESSION/ ANGER/ SADNESS

The sense of hopelessness we feel can very quickly lead to feelings of depression, sadness and anger. All of these can very quickly translate into low levels of self-esteem if we are not careful. These types of symptoms then lead to withdrawal or a projection of blame.

WITHDRAWAL/ PROJECTION OF BLAME

As we have seen, once we are depressed or feeling sad we tend to withdraw from situations. Anger mixed with sadness can be a recipe for a blaming cocktail. We get heavily into projecting blame out, and now also inwards, because there is nowhere else left to go. We are down on others and ourselves so nobody is any good, including ourselves. You can imagine what that does to the way we view ourselves.

This projection of blame in or out then leads to ongoing negative and irrational thinking and a lack of pleasant events, and so the whole cycle is repeated and becomes a *habit*. We are caught, a victim of the Victim Trap!

As you can see, this is one huge barrier to developing and building healthy levels of self-esteem within us. If you are in this trap you need to plan an escape route as soon as possible.

The longer you stay there, the more of a habit this way of reacting will become.

The following chapters will show you how to *unfreeze* this habit and refreeze more positive, adaptive habits which will assist in enhancing your level of self-esteem.

A quick exercise: Are you aware of any barriers to developing your self-esteem?

1. _____
2. _____
3. _____
4. _____
5. _____
6. _____

The previous two chapters have given you the opportunity to consider where your self-esteem has come from and what may have got in the way of you developing higher levels of it.

SUMMARY

◆ Barriers versus opportunities in life.

◆ Barriers to high levels of self-esteem:
    never had it;
    had it and lost it;
    the Victim Trap.

◆ The need to unfreeze any negative habits and refreeze positive and adaptive ones.

◆ What barriers do you recognise to the development of your self-esteem?

CHAPTER 5

Developing a healthy self-esteem

By now you know what a healthy self-esteem is, and what the barriers to having it are. The next step is to get a good healthy dose of it for yourselves, by learning to *develop* it. Like most other things in your life you can *learn* how to acquire a healthy amount of self-esteem. The main ingredient in learning to enhance your own self-esteem, to build it into one of your greatest supporters is *practise*. More than any one technique or one major issue, practise is the vital element. The techniques talked about in this book are important and you need to understand them. However, they will be quite ineffectual unless you practise them. And, of course, the more we practise them, the more useful they will become.

The trap here is that some of these techniques appear extremely obvious, and so what we often say is 'that's right, I must remember to do that!' But it often happens that we promptly *forget* to do it.

Rather than rely on our sometimes unreliable memories, we need to develop a method to help the memory. We can do this through practise. The more we practise something, the more of it goes into our memory banks and the more likely it is to come out again. Now, what do you need to practise? We'll begin by looking at some basic psychological facts.

THE BACKGROUND

As human beings there are really only three things we are doing at any one time. These are:

◆ *behaving* — engaged in actions of one type or another, be it working, playing, cooking, painting etc;

◆ *thinking* — attitudes and beliefs about the situations in your life are continuously running through your head in the form of what psychologists call 'self-talk';

◆ *emotions* — you are experiencing a range of feelings and moods. The way you are feeling will depend upon your life situation at the time, and what you are telling yourself about them at the time.

Now these three states are interactive and will have quite an effect on each other. The way we behave will affect the way we think, which will affect our emotional state, and so on. As an example, if you do something well, you may say to yourself 'that was fantastic, aren't I clever!', and you feel happy. In this case, positive actions led to positive thinking, which in turn led to positive emotions being experienced. If something we felt was negative happened, then a whole 'negative' chain reaction could have been set off.

The picture is no doubt becoming clearer. If you put your *behaviour*, *thinking* and *emotions* on automatic pilot and just let them fly themselves, anything can happen. You may do some wonderful things and your self-esteem gets a great boost. Your *behaviour*, *thinking* and *emotions* contribute to this. However, if you do not get a few wins on the board what happens to your self-esteem? It may go down as your behaviour, thinking and emotions turn negative and destructive on you.

The answer is *control*. You certainly need to be able to control your behaviour, your thinking and your emotional state. How do you do this?

TAKING CONTROL

The first thing we need to do is to make sure we have control of our mind, in particular our attitudes and beliefs about whatever is happening in our life. So let's get started and look at *attitudinal efficiency*. Make your thinking work for you!

STEP 1

Imagine that you have a tape recorder in your head. In the tape recorder is a tape, and the tape contains your memory banks. All the things that you learnt and were told as a child, and things you observed as a child are stored on that tape. In fact, all your life experiences that made it to your memory banks are stored on that tape. From the range of your experiences, you develop a whole set of beliefs about, and attitudes towards, happenings in your life. You develop a way of judging things in your life, and deciding what things you value, and you are generally able to work out how to react to life. Now, when any event is about to happen, is happening, or has just happened, the tape recorder in your head switches on and plays you messages about the event. What comes out of the tape (what is stored up there) will decide what sort of reaction or consequences you will experience from the event. So the consequences from any event will affect our behaviour, thinking and emotions.

STEP 2

The thing you then need to work out is what sort of messages are coming out of the tape recorder in your head! Are they the type of messages that enhance your self-esteem and self-image or erode it away? If a positive or desirable event happens, are the messages positive? Do they boost your self-esteem? If the events are negative or undesirable, does your self-esteem take a dive? If this is the case, don't worry, you are not alone.

STEP 3

The trick is to be able to get control over the messages that come out of that tape recorder, no matter what has happened in your life. Some, or many, of the messages coming out of your tape that may affect your self-esteem in a very negative way are:

◆ inflexible — 'I will never get it right';

◆ irrational — 'I should not make mistakes';

◆ negative — 'I am really so hopeless';

◆ stressful — 'I can't stand it';

◆ distorted — 'it's a catastrophe';

◆ upsetting — 'I'm an idiot alright'.

STEP 4

If we are going to boost our self-esteem, we need to change those negative and self-defeating messages. We need to stop that tape recorder and put far more positive messages over the top of those negative ones, so that when we switch the tape recorder back on we are far more:

◆ flexible — 'everyone makes mistakes';

◆ adaptable — 'what can I learn from all this?';

◆ rational — 'it's not the end of the world';

◆ positive — 'I did everything else pretty well';

◆ solution-orientated — 'what's the best thing for me to do now?'

You can remember what your thinking needs to be like by remembering the acronym FARPS — it's the first letter of each word listed above. So, if something happens in your life, perhaps you make a mistake or something, ask yourself if you are FARPSing. Be careful if you say it out loud!

STEP 5

Now how do we remember to start FARPSing? How do we stop that tape recorder in time, and tape messages that will enhance our self-esteem and keep our self-image intact over the top of the destructive messages? You use what I call a *thought stopping* and *thought switching* technique. Here is how it works:

1. Place a rubber band on one of your wrists. This acts as a reminder to keep an eye on what messages are coming out of your tape recorder.

2. If you find you are putting yourself down about something, flick yourself gently with the rubber band. This is purely to get your attention, *not* to punish yourself for thinking negatively.

3. Then gently say the word 'stop' to yourself. This is to stop the tape.

4. Imagine a switch in your head which switches your thinking from all the negative messages to the FARPS messages.

5. Then say four or five positive and constructive self-talks to yourself, such as 'I can cope with this, I gave it a good shot, I can't win all the time but at least I had a go'.

The thought stopping and thought switching technique can be a powerful buffer against you talking yourself into having low self-esteem and a poor self-image. This technique will allow you to talk yourself into having very healthy amounts of self-esteem, based on flexible, adaptable, rational, positive and solution-orientated messages about whatever has happened, is happening, or may happen.

Now it's time to practise. One way to start practising is to make up a situation that has or could happen to you, and start to put yourself down about it. Then using the thought stopping and thought switching technique, change the messages and actually give yourself a self-esteem boost. Here is a situation you can practise on right now.

SITUATION

You have booked a table at your favourite restaurant for a special occasion, but you are late getting to the restaurant and the table has been given to another couple. The restaurant is full.

Negative put downs you could get into:

_____

_____

_____

Now run through the thought stopping/switching technique:

_____

_____

_____

Four or five positive self-talks you could use to start FARPSing:

_____

_____

_____

_____

_____

See how easy it is! Now it's your turn to start practising. Write down an actual event that has just happened in your life, run through the self put-downs you may have said to yourself about it. Then use the thought stopping/switching technique to start FARPSing.

This is a great start towards taking control of your self-esteem and positive self-image by introducing _attitudinal efficiency_ into your life, that is, sorting your thinking out and making it positive and self-esteem enhancing. So, you have started catching yourself being negative and putting yourself down and changed that. Now the next step is to catch yourself being good.

CATCH YOURSELF BEING GOOD

We can be very quick to catch ourselves being bad and to punish ourselves. We know just how to show ourselves how stupid and crazy we can be. Just for good measure let's throw in a whole heap of self-blame and self-guilt. Do you know the feeling? If you don't, give yourself a pat on the back because you probably do *catch yourself being good*. It is vital that we focus on *what we can do* and *what we have done*, not on what we can't do and what we haven't done.

There is a type of distorted thinking style that is called *filtering*. This is where we take all the negatives and filter out all the positives from what we have done in a situation. We need to practise doing just the reverse — looking mainly at the positives and filtering out the negatives. We are not fooling ourselves when we do this. What we are doing is building on the positives so that as we go through life we keep our self-esteem and self-image intact.

It becomes terribly demotivating and debilitating emotionally when we continually point out to ourselves what we cannot do. It is motivating when we fairly consistently point out to ourselves what we have done — even the little things need to be included here. We need to make a mental note of when we:

◆ do something nice for someone;

◆ say something pleasant to someone;

◆ do a particular job or chore well;

◆ donate something to charity;

◆ find a solution to a problem;

◆ thank someone;

◆ achieve a new goal;

◆ make time to listen to someone;

◆ accept some criticism well;

◆ are honest and accepting about a mistake;

◆ stand up for ourselves;

◆ take a risk and go for it;

◆ adapt well to a change in our lives.

For each of these we need to give ourselves a pat on the back and say with confidence 'Good on me, I did do well there'. Don't let the moment pass by. You may need that store of self-esteem further down the track. Someone or something may have a go at damaging your self-esteem, but if you have plenty, you'll have plenty to fight back with.

THE SELF-TALK CYCLE

Positive self-talk is one of the keys to building and maintaining your self-esteem. The self-talk cycle works as follows.

Our self-talk will affect our self-image. This in turn has a direct effect on how we perform in life which has an effect on our self-talk. Positive self-talk has a positive effect on the cycle, negative self-talk has the reverse. A positive self-image and good personal performance or achievement will also generally have a positive effect on our self-talk.

A SELF-ESTEEM DIARY

If you find that you are having trouble focusing on your positive attributes, keep a *self-esteem diary* for a month or so. You can start it up again in the future if you need to. Buy a small notepad, and each day record three or four situations that you handled well. If you have trouble thinking of situations you handled well, jot down any situations and find the things you did well in each situation. All you need to do is record one or two situations on each page under the following headings:

Situation:

_____

_____

Things I did well:

_____

_____

_____

_____

I am an okay person because:

_____

_____

_____

_____

The last statement is there to remind us that we are okay and to spend a little time thinking about why. Life can be fairly hectic, and in the hustle and bustle of everyday living we often just plain forget to look after ourselves. The diary exercise gives us that time.

SUMMARY

◆ High positive self-esteem can be developed.

◆ Practise is a vital element.

◆ Three things as a human being we are doing at any one time:
  behaving (actions)
  thinking (attitudes and beliefs)
  emotions (feelings/moods)

◆ You can take control by using attitudinal efficiency.

◆ Remember that FARPSing is good for your self-esteem:
  F lexible;
  A daptable;
  R ational;
  P ositive;
  S olution-orientated.

◆ Use the thought-stopping and thought-switching technique to control the self-talk and the tape recorder in your head.

◆ Catch yourself being good — make a mental note.

◆ Remember the self-talk cycle.

◆ Use a self-esteem diary if you need to.

CHAPTER 6

Even more techniques

Our attitudes and self-talk are extremely important in the development of self-esteem. There is no doubt about it — they are crucial. They do need to be backed up with the right type of behaviours and actions if we are going to get the best results. If we walk around thinking positively, but behaving negatively, our self-esteem levels will gradually wear down. It will dawn on us that we are fooling ourselves. Even if we are very good at divorcing ourselves from our behaviour, telling ourselves we are okay even if our behaviour is not, the lack of positive reinforcement from doing things well will take its toll.

Of course positive thinking and positive actions do go hand in hand. However, from time to time one may need a bit more of a kick start than the other. We have just read about how to 'kick start' our thinking and positive attitudes. What about our actions?

ASSERTIVE BEHAVIOUR

Assertive behaviour is all about sticking up for yourself. There are three ways that we can interact with other people. We can be:

Passive — where we consider, on a regular basis, the needs of others before our own needs. We do things others want us to do, do things to please others and generally behave in a way that says 'I am not important but you are'. This is not going to help your self-esteem!

Aggressive — where we don't give a hoot about anybody else and act as if we are the only person with rights in the world. We bully others to get our way and become very unpleasant to be around. This type of behaviour generally does very little for developing friendships, so the feedback we get on ourselves will probably be pretty negative.

Assertive — where we develop and stick with an attitude that says ' I'm important to look after' and we act that way. We make sure our rights and needs in life are met; and while we also assist and help others meet their rights and needs as well, we do not do this at our own expense.

Being assertive is all about saying 'I am important to look after', and then sticking up for our rights and just desserts. It's a great feeling when you can say 'I don't want to do that' — it gives you a feeling of being in control of your own destiny. Pointing out to someone, in a nice way (fair and firm), that you don't agree with something also says that 'Hey, I'm important enough to have a say'. We need to be assertive if we are to have a good level of self-esteem.

A SHORT ASSERTIVENESS QUIZ

Rate yourself from 1 to 10 in terms of how much discomfort you would feel during the following:

Little discomfort	1
	2
	3
	4
Reasonably uncomfortable	5
	6
	7
	8
	9
Very uncomfortable	10

Ask a favour of a new friend _____

Start a conversation with a stranger _____

Speak up if someone pushes in front of you in a queue _____

Give someone a compliment _____

Ask for the last biscuit on the plate _____

Try to lower the price on a quote you have been given _____

Be honest with a friend even if they may not like it _____

Return damaged articles to a store _____

Ask someone to stop doing something that you are finding annoying _____

Tell someone good news about yourself _____

How assertive are you?

10–25 Well done! You really are quite assertive and stick up for yourself — as we have seen, this is very important for a good healthy level of self-esteem.

26–59 The borderline area. It is obvious that some situations cause you a reasonable amount of concern. It is useful to remember what they are and to work on them gradually.

60–100 Being assertive in many of the situations mentioned is a challenge for you. Select several situations to start working on immediately, then move on to the others.

If you have trouble being assertive, here are some hints that will help.

Pick the situations from the quiz that you feel you would like to, or need to, work on:

_____

_____

_____

_____

Notice how much discomfort you felt in those situations:

_____

_____

_____

_____

Try to give a brief summary of what you are going to do about them. How will you become more assertive?

_____

_____

_____

Now that you have had a go, here are a few extra hints on what you can do next time the situations occur:

1. Think about what you *really* want to do.
2. Say exactly what you think or what you want to do in a pleasant and firm manner.
3. Explain briefly why you came to that decision.
4. Remain calm and in control. Stick to your decision.

5. Do not argue. If pushed just restate your decision and why.
6. Give yourself a pat on the back for sticking up for yourself.

If you feel quite anxious about doing these things, you can practise them using *guided imagery*. With this technique, you relax, close your eyes and then see yourself being assertive, but pleasant. Then use some positive self-talk 'I'm doing well, I'm important to look after', then open your eyes and get on with your day.

Practise this technique in small steps, rehearsing what you need to do as you go. The benefits to your self-esteem are well worth the effort. You really do start to realise that you are the master or mistress of your own destiny and that you can enhance your self-esteem levels.

CASE STUDY

Jennifer, a mother of two young children, worked part-time and also tried to run an efficient household. Her husband was not very helpful with the housework or the daily running of the home. Jennifer had been juggling most of the load since the children had been born. She finally decided things needed to change.

Jennifer talked to her husband about how she was feeling and the pressure she felt at having to juggle so many things. She had two solutions, and one had to be implemented. Someone else had to clean the house or her husband had to help her do it on Saturday mornings until it was finished. They agreed to hire someone to come in and clean the house once a week.

Jennifer had not raised the matter earlier because she felt some guilt about the fact that she found the demands of motherhood coupled with paid employment too much. She was also reluctant to pay a person to clean the house, because she felt the family may not be able to afford such a 'luxury'.

EFFECTIVE COMMUNICATION

This is another very important behaviour, and one that is critical for self-esteem. When we communicate in a clear, open and honest manner we tend to feel good about ourselves. When we don't, our sense of well-being is not so good. The basics of effective communication are levelling, listening and validating.

LEVELLING

Levelling means telling it like it is, telling other people how you feel in an assertive and positive manner. Levelling lets other people know exactly where you stand. It takes the guesswork out of the situation, so that others do not have to guess where you are at or where you are coming from. Not levelling can put unnecessary strain on relationships as well as making you feel uneasy about yourself. When we don't level we tend to perceive ourselves as weak, and it's hard to have high self-esteem when you have that perception of yourself.

LISTENING

Being a good listener is more than pointing your ears in the right direction! It means showing others, with your actions and attitudes, that you are interested in what they are saying. Not butting in, hearing them out and letting them know that you heard them are crucial listening skills. Good listening also means clarifying if you are unsure what someone else is saying.

Yap, Yap

VALIDATING

Validating means accepting that what someone says about their feelings they actually feel. When we validate we say something like 'I can see you feel really upset by what has happened'. We may not agree or understand why they are feeling that way, however, we acknowledge that they are. You can perhaps point out that you do not agree with them, while letting them know that you appreciate that they are feeling a particular way.

We feel much better about ourselves when we are communicating well with others, understanding and being understood as well.

A CHECKLIST OF EFFECTIVE COMMUNICATION SKILLS

Do you:

◆ remain relaxed;

◆ maintain eye contact;

◆ smile and nod;

◆ say what is on your mind;

◆ remain assertive, not passive or aggressive;

◆ let the other person finish talking;

◆ try and empathise with and understand the person;

◆ contribute to conversations;

◆ ask questions about and of others;

◆ speak slowly and clearly;

◆ ask for others' opinions;

◆ admit when you are wrong and accept criticism;

◆ always look for a solution?

PROBLEM-SOLVING AND SETTING GOALS

The resolution of a problem is a major self-esteem booster, and is closely linked to setting and achieving goals. To help us along the way, here is a quick and effective problem-solving technique.

◆ Define the problem — Knowing exactly what the problem is, is not always straightforward. For example, we may see the problem as the fact that we are unhappy. This is too unclear. We need to look at why we are unhappy, and what we can do about it. And we need to look at those particular things that we feel are making us unhappy. So the idea is to break the problem down as much as possible — 'I spend too little time on pleasant activities'.

◆ Consider all solutions — Write down all the ways you can think of to resolve the situations. Strange or unusual ones are allowed at this stage. If you get stuck, ask others!

◆ Evaluate the solutions — What are the good and bad points of the solutions you came up with? List these down.

◆ Select a solution — Given your evaluation, what is the best thing for you to do right now? It may not be the very best solution if it costs too much money, or would take too much time. It is the most practical solution at this time

◆ Plan your attack — How are you going to go about implementing the solution? What are the steps that are necessary to go through? Try to achieve one plan of attack at a time.

◆ Try your plan and test its effectiveness — Now get in and do it, monitoring and keeping an eye on it as you go. If you find you need to change aspects of the solution, that is fine. Don't give yourself a hard time over it, just get on and make the changes, and perhaps the way you are going about things.

Effective problem-solving and goal setting leads to better achievements, which leads to higher self-esteem, which leads to attempting more in life. There is no question that it is certainly good for you.

SUMMARY

◆ We need to be assertive, not passive or aggressive with our behaviour.

◆ Effective communication means:
>   levelling;
>   listening;
>   validating.

◆ Proper problem-solving and goal setting leads to more and more achievements, so:
1. define the problem;
2. consider all solutions;
3. evaluate the solutions;
4. select a solution;
5. plan your attack;
6. try and test your plan.

CHAPTER 7

Benefits of having high self-esteem

This is a very important chapter of the book. It may lead some people to go back and re-read some of the earlier chapters. Considering the benefits of high self-esteem draws our attention to just how important this is for us to develop a high quality of life. It is not difficult to imagine what the benefits of having low self-esteem are! In fact, let's consider some of these first.

POOR SELF-IMAGE

This is when we don't particularly like ourselves. We may need constantly to seek assurances from other people that we are okay. That leads to doing what others want us to do so that we get their approval. We forget about what we want in life, and apologise for ourselves. We say things like 'I know this probably sounds silly, but I think . . .'. Talk about the ultimate self put down! With a poor self-image, we are constantly comparing ourselves to others and gauging how well we are doing in life by how well others are doing. As soon as we see someone who is doing better than us, we feel like a dismal failure.

Once again, what happened to the focus on what *we* want in life? We don't take risks, try new things or meet new people because we feel we are so hopeless or so boring that others would not enjoy our company! It may sound like I am exaggerating, but this kind of response happens when we have low self-esteem. Sometimes, it gets out of control, we don't like ourselves so we get into *anorexic* or *bulimic* behaviours, dieting out of control, in order to keep some control over our lives. Unfortunately some of this very maladaptive response to low self-esteem can have dire consequences and, in extreme cases, even lead to death.

DEPRESSION

It is quite normal to feel a bit down, to wonder what it is really all about and to get the blues for short periods of time. Even people with high self-esteem get a bit down from time to time. However, when our self-esteem is quite low we are far more predisposed to getting the very serious clinical depressive disorders. These involve feeling bad, or guilty, or like you are being punished for something. A loss of meaning in life and a lack of pleasant events in life can result, and it is not uncommon to wonder if you will get over it or if life is really worth going on with. Unfortunately for some, suicide is the end result. Others will attempt suicide to let others know just how badly they are dealing with life, or to get back at others because they blame them for the way they are feeling.

LACK OF ACHIEVEMENT

It goes without saying that when we have low levels of self-esteem, we don't believe we can achieve things, so we don't try. As has been mentioned earlier, it is as though we write a script for ourselves (a life script), which says all the way through it that we will not, and cannot achieve. The sad thing is that we then live out this script and follow it, much the same as an actor would follow the script of a play. A vicious cycle is set up of 'I can't achieve', so you don't achieve, which adds more fuel to the fire — 'See, I knew I couldn't do it'.

THE POOR ME TRAP

This is a cracker! How many of us from time to time figure that life has dealt us a rather poor hand? We feel that life is not fair, how could this happen to such a nice person like me?

Well, from time to time and for very short periods it is

acceptable to feel like this. There are people, however, who live their lives like that, who constantly feel that someone has had a go at them. People like this blame their parents or friends for why their life is a misery. And they often blame themselves, believing that they are so helpless that they are unable to make a go of it! Why do they do this? Yes you guessed it, *low self-esteem*. Because they are not confident that they can make a go of life, they resort to the 'poor me' syndrome as a maladaptive way of giving themselves an excuse. Does it ring a bell? If it does, don't panic. The techniques you have read about in this book will help you to turn all that around. You, and all of us are far too important to let that type of thing permeate or take over our lives, so *control* it, do not let it control you!

LIFE WASTAGE

At the end of the day, low self-esteem adds up to a waste of life. We need to think seriously about the fact that life is not a trial run, and that we only have one shot at it. *So make the best of it!* You cannot give your life the best shot if you have low self-esteem. Anxiety, fear, lack of confidence, negative thinking, useless actions all add to the wastage. Develop an attitude which says 'no wastage for me', and give your life some meaningful pursuits.

Now for the benefits.

After reading and practising the techniques outlined in this book, these are the benefits you have to look forward to. If you are already doing well, practising the techniques will help you to reap even more benefits for yourself.

POSITIVE SELF-IMAGE

The 'I like me' syndrome is extremely good for you. You are not saying that you are the best or smartest person in the world, you are simply stating that you like yourself. Let's face it, you have to live with yourself 24 hours a day seven days a week. As we saw earlier in this chapter, it's extremely difficult if you don't like yourself.

With a positive self-image you are in a state of well-being most of the time. You are relaxed and confident, pleasant and helpful to others, solution-orientated if a challenge occurs in your life. You are generally very happy to be alive and to be who you are. This is irrespective of what you look like, how tall you are or how you are built — all those things in life that you have little control over. You need to *accept* those things and get on with life, making the most out of what you drew in the lottery of life, and controlling those things that are controllable.

ACHIEVEMENT FOCUSED

One of the great benefits of having high self-esteem is that we focus on meaningful pursuits in our life, things that will add to the overall quality of our lives. We don't worry about doing things that are not important, instead we plan and work on those things that will make a difference. We look at what we can do and build on that, not at what we can't do or haven't done.

We have a feeling and an image of ourselves as achievers. Remember that life script I talked about earlier? With a good self-image you write a life script that is full of 'I can . . . I will . . . I am able to . . . watch me go'. We then tend to live out

that life script. As I have said earlier, *success builds success*. You need to make the decisions about what you want to be successful at in life. That is your choice.

A BALANCED LIFESTYLE

A healthy level of self-esteem will lead to a far better balance in life. Adequate time will be spent in vocational or work activities, intimate activities with people you are very close to, social activities with friends, and community interests and leisure and recreational pursuits. People who feel good about themselves do not allow themselves to fall into a 'martyr' syndrome. They do not hinge their self-image on having to be the boss, or earning a million dollars a year. They are happy with who they are. So they spread their time doing and achieving things across the whole spectrum of life. They are also less vulnerable if they miss out in one area, because they are still doing well in the other areas of their lives.

A BUFFER AGAINST THE NASTIES

Yes, indeed, one of the most important parts that self-esteem plays in our lives is to buffer us against those nasties that can creep in upon us if we leave our guard down. With high self-esteem we are buffered against those minor psychological symptoms such as:

◆ irritability;

◆ moodiness;

◆ the blues;

◆ intolerance;

◆ fatigue;

◆ sleep problems;

◆ feeling out of sorts.

High self-esteem can also help us fight the more serious situations, like:

◆ clinical depression;

◆ alcohol or drug abuse;

◆ violence;

◆ burnout/nervous breakdown;

◆ phobias or panic attacks;

◆ high blood pressure;

◆ over-eating/under-eating;

◆ tension/migraine headaches.

It comes back to that old saying 'an ounce of prevention is worth a pound of cure'. The disorders mentioned above are certainly treatable, but some require quite lengthy treatment, so preventing them occurring in the first place is the way to go. When we feel good about ourselves and are acting and thinking in that positive manner, it is far less likely that the psychological disorders will creep in, or build up within us. So protect yourself — work on that self-esteem level and don't stop until you can look yourself in the eye and say 'Yes, I like me'. Even practising saying it helps.

SUMMARY

◆ Low self-esteem leads to:
   poor self-image;
   depression;
   lack of achievement;
   the 'poor me' trap;
   life wastage.

◆ Benefits of high self-esteem:
   positive self-image;
   achievement focused;
   a balanced lifestyle;
   a buffer against the nasties.

◆ Remember that an ounce of prevention is worth a pound of cure.

◆ It's important that you like yourself.

CHAPTER 8

Maintaining your gains

It is all very well to embrace something in life and decide that 'yes' I am going to give that a really good go. We can start off very motivated, enthusiastic and champing at the bit to get into it. However, what happens a week, month, a year down the track? Will we still be on the ball and doing well? Focused on what it is we need to do? Or will we have let it all slip, and be back into those habits that are not helping our quality of life at all.

If you are like this, don't despair, even if your life is full of those episodes where you thought something was well worth while, got right into it, only to find that in a short period of time you were back to your old ways. Psychologically what we are often looking for in life is a quick fix — something that will work with very little effort, something that will work right now. It's what psychologists refer to as the principle of *immediate gratification* — we have to have our needs met immediately. When starting something new, we often only focus on the short-term and forget to set a *vision* for how we want the future to be.

So let's have a look at what you need to do to ensure your efforts are rewarded over time.

HAVE A VISION

When thinking about and setting our goals to achieve high levels of self-esteem, we need to develop a clear vision or picture of what we want to be doing in that area 12 months down the track. How do we see ourselves behaving, thinking and what would we like to be achieving? What sort of things do we see ourselves doing to maintain the high level of self-esteem we have acquired? It is helpful to spend some time actually imagining how we will be feeling, and how we will be interacting with other people. Imagine your feelings of confidence!

So let's take this opportunity to set that vision for yourself. Remember that you need to make positive lifestyle changes for life, not just for the moment. You want these changes to become habits, a positive addiction if you like.

The self-esteem vision I have for myself, is:

_____

_____

_____

_____

Now add to your vision a *mission statement* — that is, why you want to do this.

My *mission* in maintaining high levels of self-esteem is so that I will:

_____

_____

_____

You now have what is known as a *vision* and *mission* statement for yourself regarding your self-esteem levels. It is a good reminder as to why you are going to pay attention to this very important area of your life. Well done.

KEEP YOUR EYE ON THE BALL

This is an analogy taken from the sporting arena. If you want to catch a ball cleanly in netball, or mark a football confidently and firmly, you need to keep your eye on the ball. Take your eye off the ball, and you stand the chance of dropping it, fumbling it or missing it altogether. It is the same with anything in life. If we forget about it, don't worry about it, take our eye off it, we will tend to lose it, mess it up or start to lose confidence in our ability to do it. So from now on, your self-esteem is something you need to think about and analyse from time to time. There is no need to go overboard with it so that you become obsessed with self-esteem, and where your whole life revolves around boosting your self-esteem, like those people who become exercise fanatics — they eventually burn out on it or do themselves some harm. On a regular basis we need to revisit some of the exercises in this book to see how we are going. Can we continue as we are going, or do we need to modify particular things about our behaviour and attitudes?

Be careful about taking for granted that once you are reasonable at something you will always be reasonable at it. You can get a bit rusty over time, and you can forget important aspects or issues about what you are doing. Take the example

of showering. After your shower this morning (or evening), you feel nice and clean, fresh, germ-free, and you smell great! Does that mean you will never have to shower again because you will always now be clean, free of germs and smelling like a flower. Obviously it doesn't, and in fact tomorrow you will go through the same routine again.

It is exactly the same with self-esteem. Just because we may have it at a great level today, does not automatically ensure it will still be there tomorrow. We need to work on it tomorrow to ensure we still have it there and get all those benefits from it.

PRACTISE, PRACTISE, PRACTISE

Yes, this has been mentioned before and needs to be mentioned again and again. There is nothing quite as important in continuing to do something well in life as practise on a regular basis. How did the top tennis players or the top musicians in the world today get where they are? Maybe a little 'natural' talent and lots of practice day after day. How do they stay there? They practise day after day. Why do they bother? The rewards are worth it.

It is exactly the same for the rest of us. We must look at what we wish to achieve and decide that it is worth it, and then practise the techniques regularly so that we stay good at keeping our self-esteem and self-image high.

Like practising for anything, we need to know what to do, how to do it and where to get some coaching if we need it. Chapter 12 looks at extra 'coaching' that is available for you if you feel you need it.

THE COMPANY YOU KEEP

Many years ago psychologists began looking at the question of *free will* and *determinism*. Free will means we can do anything we wish to, while determinism means that our actions will be determined by what is happening around us. The psychologists tried to work out which concept was actually the case for human beings, and decided that human behaviour was a mixture of the two — they called this *reciprocal determinism*.

What we need to be aware of is that our environment *and* the people in it will make a difference in how we see ourselves. So we need to be careful who we have in our circle of friends and who we mix with for social and leisure pursuits. If we mix with people who are very negative and cynical and who put us or themselves down, then that behaviour may eventually rub off on us. It's the same as where we live. If we live in an untidy 'dive' we treat it that way, not bothering to look after it. If it is a nice tidy place we are more likely to treat it in a similar fashion.

It is the same with our friends or support group. Things to look for in friends or a support group include:

◆ positive, optimistic attitudes to life;

◆ people who like themselves, and do not abuse themselves (too much alcohol etc);

◆ people who notice your positives and comment on them;

◆ achievers in life;

◆ people who have a good balance in their lives;

◆ people who are friendly and respectful to others;

◆ people you can learn from and look up to.

Spend a lot of time with people who *value* you, and listen to what they are saying about you.

People who are the opposite of this are the ones who are likely to help lower your self-esteem rather than enhance it, so be careful whenever you are around them. Develop and work at keeping a very good supply of positive, optimistic friends who you can go through life with. This is essential if you are going to maintain good levels of self-esteem.

TOLERANCE AND PATIENCE

Both these qualities are essential to maintain your self-esteem. The old saying 'Rome wasn't built in a day' applies well to self-esteem. It takes time to get a good healthy level of self-esteem, and if we expect it all too quickly we may become somewhat demotivated along the way. Patience and tolerance of ourselves and others is very important. Try not to criticise yourself or others too quickly, and don't allow others to criticise you on a regular basis or too often. Keep mistakes in perspective — don't dwell on them, try to understand why they occurred and what you can do about them. Few mistakes you or others make are real catastrophes, however our reactions may be catastrophic if we are not careful.

If someone is in the habit of regularly pointing out your mistakes, or what they don't agree with, try this technique: stop them when they start to criticise and tell them you will be happy to accept the criticism but only after they have said two positive things about you.

If they can't, don't allow them to criticise, or don't listen to the criticism — they haven't been observing well enough. If they do say two nice things, listen to the criticism and thank them for taking the time to discuss the issue with you.

By doing this you tend to keep people honest. If they have been observing you correctly, then they will certainly be able to come up with two positives, even if those positives are only small things. This technique allows us to restore our self-esteem levels before we get the criticism which may tear at it a little.

SELF-MOTIVATION

Having a great group of friends who value you and say nice things about you can provide you with a lot of external motivation. However, the motivation to do well at anything that is most controllable comes from within you, through:

◆ positive self-talk — psyching yourself up not out;

◆ setting small steps to your goals and rewarding yourself for achieving each step;

◆ catching yourself being good;

◆ keeping a good balance of activities in your life;

◆ achieving your goals;

◆ relaxing and pampering yourself at times;

◆ looking at the bright side of life;

◆ setting a positive life script for yourself to follow.

Go for it! Make sure you read this chapter again in a few months' time, just to make sure you are on the ball.

SUMMARY

◆ Be aware of your need for immediate gratification.

◆ Set a *vision* of where you want to be in 12 months' time.

◆ Have a *mission* — why do you want to be there?

◆ Keep your eye on the ball — focus on developing your self-esteem.

◆ Practise, practise, practise.

◆ Look at the company you keep. Positive friends and support groups are very important.

◆ Develop tolerance and patience.

◆ Be self-motivating — catch yourself being good.

CHAPTER 9

You know you're successful when . . .

How do you know you're successfully maintaining a high level of self-esteem? Some of the effects of having high self-esteem talked about in Chapter 7 will certainly be happening, along with some of the issues mentioned in this chapter. It is reassuring to be able to recognise the signs of success. It helps take some of the pressure off and it keeps you motivated.

So what are the signs that you are successfully maintaining high levels of self-esteem?

VALUING YOURSELF

It's important to know your own value and not have to rely on others to tell you that you are worthwhile. You need to be a self-contained unit. It is so critical, because you just never know when an uncontrollable event may happen in your life — a chronic illness, the death of a loved one, the break up of a relationship.

The more you value yourself and your quality of life, the quicker you will recover. Because you value yourself, you will not allow yourself to fall into a Victim Trap or a 'poor me' syndrome, and you will effectively rebuild a new life for yourself. Valuing yourself is a sure sign of being successful.

CHALLENGES AND CHANGES

When you can roll with the punches, as they say, and handle the challenges that this great journey of life hands us, you are successful. When you can adapt readily to changes in your work or personal life and the changes that occur as we go through life, you are successful. The different roles you will play — lover, worker, partner, friend, spouse, parent, grandparent all require a high level of self-esteem, if we are to adapt to them well. As we have seen, if you are a parent with low self-esteem, you are likely to pass that on to your children, so always remember that high self-esteem not only helps you, but helps those closest to you.

HUMOUR

Another sign of high self-esteem is a good sense of humour. When you can take the seriousness out of life, relax and not always have to be right or be on top of everything, you probably *are* on top of everything! This is a good sign that your self-esteem is in such good condition that you do not need to be *proving* yourself all the time.

Proving ourselves from time to time is good for us, but it should not be done constantly. Being able to laugh at the silly things you do is important. Seeing the humour in life means you feel at ease letting your guard down and having some fun. You are not afraid of what others may think of you — this is a very good way to be.

RESPONSIBILITY

Taking responsibility for what you do in life is also important and is another sign of your maturing self-esteem. Refuse to take on self-blame and guilt. If you mess up on something admit it, accept it, and rectify it if you can and want to.

When we can take responsibility for things in our lives, there is little need for defensiveness, telling fibs or dissolving into an emotional mess when things go wrong. We face up to our problems and get on with life. Guilt and self-blame just rip away your self-esteem in huge chunks, leaving you very exposed. Others may try to use guilt against you, so don't allow them to get away with it. Explain to them that you know what they are up to and ask them to move on.

ASSERTIVE

This has been mentioned before, and once again is a clear signal of self-esteem. If we can stick up for ourselves and ask for what we want, and refuse to do what we don't want to, our self-esteem is pretty much intact. A person with high self-esteem and who is assertive does not have to be passive or aggressive in the way they go about things. They will not cop it sweet, nor will they find it necessary to bully others to get what they want. They stick up for their own rights, while recognising others also have rights. They speak up and put their ideas and their thoughts on a subject forward.

EFFICIENCY

Another sign is the ability to be efficient, that is to do the right things *right* in life. With high self-esteem you will settle for nothing less, because you realise that your time is too important to waste. Wasting your time means wasting your life! Being efficient across all areas of life is a very good indicator of high self-esteem, because you will not allow yourself to become a martyr in one area, and neglect the others. There is a very real sense of being the master or mistress of your own destiny.

SENSE OF BELONGING

With high self-esteem comes a sense of belonging. Whether it be your family, peers and friends, workplace, community or country, you feel a real sense of belonging and you therefore become a contributing member. You involve yourself in the activities — you don't withdraw or avoid. This, of course, reinforces your own sense that you are a worthwhile person. A very positive cycle of events is set up.

SUMMARY

- Recognising the signs of success is a great source of ongoing motivation.
- Signposts of success are:
    valuing yourself;
    enjoying challenges and changes;
    humour;
    ability to take responsibility;
    being assertive;
    being efficient — doing the right things *right*;
    a sense of belonging.

CHAPTER 10

Living with someone with low self-esteem

This certainly can be a challenge for anyone! The major consideration here is that you look after yourself first, with the person you are living with following a close second. This does mean that you are selfish or inconsiderate, but that you are not going to become a victim to anyone else or anything else in life. So you need to develop a *buffer zone* between yourself and the effects of the other person, other people or other things. You certainly do not have to cut yourself off from that person, although in some cases, this may well become necessary.

The following diagram was first developed by psychologists who came up with a branch of psychology called *transactional analysis*, or T.A., as it is commonly known. It is one way of explaining the interactions between people, how they communicate and interact with one another. Study the diagram below.

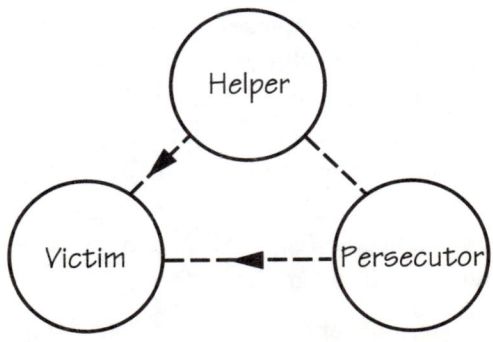

It is very important for us all to be aware of the 'victim-helper-persecutor' triangle, because it can have relevance to many situations in life. When we see someone who is a 'victim' we can go into a 'helper' role. Our desire is to help the victim get rid of the 'persecutor', which is, of course, a positive thing to do. So, what do these terms mean?

Helper — someone who wants to assist another to do better in life.

Victim — a person who is having trouble coping with something in life.

Persecutor — the person or thing the victim is having troubles with. This can be anything at all.

If you assist the victim with advice and support, and that person gets on top of things and learns how to deal with the persecutor effectively, all is well. However, if the victim does not get any better, then a number of things can occur.

1. You can wear yourself out trying to help the victim, and so end up a victim yourself.
2. The victim turns on you saying your help was useless, and in fact they now feel worse! The victim is now persecuting you. How do you feel?
3. You can blame yourself because the victim is no better, and so start to persecute yourself.
4. The victim gets no better, so you start to persecute the victim as well, saying things like 'You're hopeless, you don't want to get any better . . . you're just feeling sorry for yourself'.

In spite of the fact that you started off with the best intentions of helping the victim, these things may occur. You can see how this applies to someone you are close to if they have low self-esteem. If you see them as a victim and you come in as the helper, you have to be very careful, so that the points listed above do not happen!

This is where you need a *buffer zone* to make sure you remain a helper, and do not end up a victim or a persecutor yourself.

What goes in the buffer zone?

◆ keep up your own fulfilling lifestyle;

◆ remind yourself you cannot help any one in the long-term, you can only help them to help themselves;

◆ have a routine in life you enjoy;

◆ have lots of positive friends;

◆ keep up your hobbies, interests, holidays;

◆ keep your self-esteem high.

The most important thing to remember is that in the long run, you cannot help anyone, you can only help them to help themselves.

This is very important for the other person, not just for yourself. What happens if instead of being a helper, you fall into a *rescuer* role? When we consistently rescue others, they do not need to take responsibility for learning how to help themselves. So we may in fact be helping them to stay in the victim role!

Let's see if there is situation in your life that you need to be aware of.

Helper role — I am in a helper role with: (use a false name if you wish)

_____

The victim — this person is a victim because he or she cannot:

_____

_____

_____

_____

The persecutor — in this case the persecutor is:

_____

_____

I try to assist the victim by:

_____

_____

_____

_____

By doing this, I now realise I am being a — select one — helper, rescuer, victim or persecutor:

The reason I feel I am being this is because I am:

_____

_____

What I need to put in my buffer zone to ensure I stay there is:

_____

_____

_____

I am important to look after because:

_____

_____

_____

_____

_____

Okay, now that you are looking after yourself, it is time to consider what you can do to help the person to help himself or herself.

First, *be with* the person, and then try and *do with* the person. This means:

Be with — listen to, and really try to understand where the person is coming from. Why are they having problems and how are they feeling about those problems?

This is best done several times, each time making sure you:

◆ allow enough time — don't rush things or the person will feel that you don't really care;

◆ let the person speak — your job is to listen and try to understand what the person is experiencing;

◆ clarify when necessary — make sure you ask for clarification or more explanation if you are unsure of something;

◆ don't make judgments — try not to get ahead of the person, or 'read their mind'.

When you feel you understand, and the person has had an adequate chance to talk about their feelings, move to the next step.

Doing with — after being with the person, you are ready to work on an action plan with that person, that is, to *do* with them.

If formulating a plan of attack to rectify what is happening, you are helping to find a solution. In other words, devise a problem-solving strategy:

1. Define the problem — what is the challenge they have?
2. You both know how they feel about it.
3. Brainstorm solutions — what are the possibilities?
4. Consider the good and bad points of each solution.
5. Select a solution.
6. Plan an attack — how can it be implemented?
7. How will you assist the person?
8. Review — will what has been decided work?
9. When will you get together to see how things are going?
10. Give yourself a pat on the back for working on a solution.

As the person is working on the plan, make sure you:

◆ praise them for all efforts made, that is catch them being good;

◆ if you need to point out that they are off the track, start by running through some positive steps they have made;

◆ let them drive the plan — do not take over, unless they really get lost;

◆ keep your lifestyle going as well.

GENERAL HINTS FOR HELPERS AND SUPPORTERS

◆ Praise to criticism ratio needs to be at least 3 to 1.

◆ Does the person just need an ear, or advice at that time?

◆ Don't mind read or make value judgments.

◆ Don't try and be an expert if you are not.

◆ Get expert assistance if you need it.

◆ Becoming overly emotional will probably make things worse.

◆ Be careful of the rescuer, victim and persecutor roles.

◆ Communicate supportively and honestly.

◆ Show tolerance, but do not martyr yourself.

◆ Share any frustrations you have, and let the person know they are not to blame for them.

◆ Accept responsibility for your own feelings of frustration and do not blame the other person. Remember you are electing to stay there and assist them, so own the decision, you made it. Nobody can force you to stay or support.

SUMMARY

◆ Be aware of the helper-victim-persecutor roles.

◆ Fill up your buffer zone.

◆ Be careful of the rescuer role.

◆ Be with — understand what is happening with the person, and then:

◆ Do with — assist the person to establish an action plan.

◆ Remember the general hints for helpers and supporters.

CHAPTER 11

Memory joggers — personal action plan

This chapter allows you to review those very important issues talked about in this book, so that you have a very good overall understanding of the big picture in terms of your self-esteem. As we are now aware, self-esteem is a very important area of life because it is the foundation that our quality of life is built upon. If it is in bad shape, unstable or unreliable, then anything else we attempt in life will be built on that unstable base.

Don't get stressed about the whole issue, come at it as you hopefully would with any other challenge in your life — with realistic goal setting, enthusiasm, a sense of adventure and optimism.

The way to use this chapter is to:

◆ attempt to answer the questions by filling in the spaces;

◆ check your answers by going back to the relevant chapters;

◆ find the answer by going to the relevant chapter;

◆ be a general revision of the whole book.

A MEMORY TEST

So, let us now test out our memory and set an action plan for ourselves as we do it.

1. Define self-esteem:

_____

_____

_____

_____

2. How do you know when you have good self-esteem levels?

_____

_____

_____

_____

3. Where did your present level of self-esteem come from?

_____

_____

_____

_____

4. Are you aware of any barriers to your self-esteem?

_____

_____

_____

5. List four ways of raising your self-esteem:

_____

_____

_____

_____

6. What are the benefits to you of having high self-esteem?

_____

_____

_____

_____

7. What do you need to do to maintain high self-esteem?

_____

_____

_____

_____

8. How do you know when you are being successful?

_____

_____

_____

_____

9. What are five things to be aware of when living with someone with low self-esteem?

a. _____

b. _____

c. _____

d. _____

e. _____

10. Why are you important to look after?

_____

_____

_____

_____

Well done. It's great that you made time to fill in the blanks, to take control of your own life. Good on you!

CHAPTER 12

Sources of assistance

WHY SEEK EXTRA PROFESSIONAL HELP?

I have been reinforcing throughout this book, that you are important to look after. If you feel you do need extra assistance to raise your self-esteem, then do it. Self-help books like this one are great, but there are times when extra advice and counselling from a qualified and trained professional in the area is necessary. The extra professional help can ensure that you do get control over your self-esteem. Counselling, if approached in the right manner, is a definite sign of personal strength.

If you go along with the attitude that you will get some help so you can help yourself, you are on the right track. You need to hang onto that attitude, even if initially you feel you need someone stronger than yourself to rely on.

All we need to do now then, is to ensure that you obtain the right advice, support or counselling. This means you need to know what type of counsellors to see and where to find them.

WHO DO YOU SEE?

For assistance with self-esteem, you have the choice of either:

◆ individual assistance; or
◆ group workshops.

Either can be very effective. It really depends on which way you would like to go:

Individual assistance — Here the focus is fully on you and your situation. You have the undivided attention of the counsellor, who will provide a very personal focus on what is happening to you, how you feel about it and what you can do about it.

Group workshops — Here the focus is on shared experiences. Each person in the group will have a turn to speak. Group workshops can assist you to realise you are not alone in the way you are feeling. They allow for the practise of techniques through activities such as role plays, and they can also act as a support group.

INDIVIDUAL ASSISTANCE

CLINICAL OR COUNSELLING PSYCHOLOGISTS

Psychologists are well trained in the whole area of helping people to develop higher levels of self-esteem. They can provide advice, counselling, therapy and support for you. Make sure the psychologist has training in the cognitive-behavioural forms of counselling and therapy.

Make sure that any psychologist you choose is registered in your State.

Psychologists are either in private practice or work for hospitals or government organisations such as Community Health Services.

SOCIAL WORKERS

Some social workers are also well trained in the area of self-esteem training. There are a few in private practice, but most social workers work for various hospital and government institutions. Make sure the social worker is a member of the Australian Association of Social Workers.

GROUP WORKSHOPS

Workshops are often conducted by the Community Health or Health Promotion Units of large hospitals or Area Health Services. Group workshop leaders are either professionals, or trained volunteers. Trained volunteers are fine, just enquire about the volunteers' training and who supervises them. Make sure you feel comfortable with their level of training.

HOW TO FIND THEM

Psychologists are located under P in your State's Yellow Pages. These are generally psychologists in private practice, so you will pay for their services. Fees vary widely from about $60 — $140 per session. The fee recommended by the Australian Psychological Society was around $140 an hour at the time this book was written. To check, you can always call the society on Freecall 1800 333 497. Remember, you sometimes really do get what you pay for. Beware of the cheapies!

Community Health Centres, mental health teams and your local large hospital may also have psychologists on staff who provide services to the general community. These services are generally free. The Health Promotion Unit at your local hospital may also have details of self-esteem workshops and seminars that are generally quite cheap and quite well run.

If you find you are feeling desperate with your low self-esteem, or that you are overcome with guilt or hopelessness, services such as Lifeline provide an Australia-wide emergency contact and are generally very supportive indeed. There is a list of these community services in the beginning of the white pages in your local phone book.

Your local general practitioner will also be able to refer you to a good psychologist.

Social workers can be found under S in the Yellow Pages and many also work for community and government agencies. Your local hospital will probably have one or two on staff, who provide services to the community.

If you are in employment, your organisation may have free confidential counselling services available through an Employee Assistance Program. You may also be able to arrange for self-esteem, assertiveness or self-development workshops.

BEWARE!

Medication to help with low self-esteem is a very dangerous path to go down indeed. Sometimes, for disorders where a low self-esteem factor is involved, medication in the short-term may be useful while you are getting help to raise your self-image. It is very dangerous to take medication to try to *escape* from your problems.

Medication can be dependency building and will do nothing constructive in the long-term. If your doctor has you on medication for low self-esteem, get a second opinion as soon as possible, and arrange to see a well qualified psychologist.

If you have developed a severe depressive disorder or your self-esteem is down due to a psychotic disorder, then work closely with your doctor or psychiatrist on monitoring your medication. This is relevant only to a very few people, as most people with low self-esteem do not have and will not get those disorders.

LONG-TERM PSYCHOANALYSIS

Generally speaking, this is a waste of time, energy and money. There are far more effective interventions for people with low self-esteem to which the research testifies quite clearly.

Beware of the professionals who tell you they need to see you three times a week or for a two to five year period. It's best to stay away from them. Definitely get a second opinion as to what to do if you find yourself in that situation.

FRINGE DWELLERS

There are many so-called therapists and counsellors lurking around out there. Some are well meaning and some just outright charlatans, ready to fleece you. The techniques these people use are often aimed at fostering dependency on them so you go back time and time again. These types of people often prey on you when you are most emotionally vulnerable. Please seek the advice of trusted long time friends or professionals before signing up. Some fringe dwellers operate out of various cults or religious style organisations, so be careful.

REMINDER

Remember that you are important to look after. If you need professional assistance, go get it!

Take very good care of yourself, and work on enhancing the quality of your life. It certainly is worth it.

FURTHER READING

Brecht, G. *Sorting out Goals*, Prentice Hall, Sydney, 1996.

Brecht, G. *Sorting out Stress*, Prentice Hall, Sydney, 1996.

Brecht, G. *Sorting out Worry*, Prentice Hall, Sydney, 1996.

Burns, D. *The Feeling Good Handbook*, William Morrow, New York, 1989.

Ellis, A. *How to stubbornly refuse to make yourself miserable about anything, yes, anything!* Pan Macmillan, Sydney, 1991.

Montgomery, R. and Morris, L. *Living with Anxiety*, Lothian, Melbourne, 1992.

Seligman, M. *What You Can Change and What You Can't: The Complete Guide to Successful Self-improvement*, Random House, Sydney, 1994.

INDEX